A New True Book

THE MOHAWK

By Jill Duvall

CHILDRENS PRESS®
CHICAGO

Wooden carving of a Mohawk head

PHOTO CREDITS

The Bettmann Archive—9, 15, 16 (2 photos), 22, 30 (2 photos), 34

© Reinhard Brucker—10 (3 photos), 17, 20 (2 photos), 21 (2 photos), 24 (right), 25 (3 photos)

C.P. Cushing/H. Armstrong Roberts—32 (left), 33

Historical Pictures Service—19

Courtesy of The New York Historical Society, New York City—32 (right)

North Wind Picture Archives—4

Root Resources—© Jim West—41, 45

Photograph Courtesy of Smithsonian Institution National Museum of the American Indian—14 (Neg #21692)

SuperStock International, Inc.—13, 24 (left) © Vernon Sigl, Cover, 7; © Truxton Hosley, 2

Valan—© Kennon Cooke, 26; © Harold Rosenberg, 28 (2 photos), 37, 38, 39, 40, 43 (3 photos)

COVER: "Hail to the Sun" Mohawk Indian Memorial—Charlemont, MA.

Library of Congress Cataloging-in-Publication Data

Duvall, Jill D.
The Mohawk / by Jill D. Duvall.
p. cm. — (A New true book)
Includes index.
Summary: Highlights the history and some of the political and social traditions of the Mohawk tribe and Iroquois confederation.
ISBN 0-516-01115-4
1. Mohawk Indians—Juvenile literature. 2. Iroquois Indians—Juvenile literature. [1. Mohawk Indians. 2. Iroquois Indians. 3. Indians of North America.] I. Title.
E99.M8D88 1991 90-21166
973'.04975—dc20 CIP
AC

Printed in the United States of America.
1 2 3 4 5 6 7 8 9 10 R 00 99 98 97 96 95 94 93 92 91

TABLE OF CONTENTS

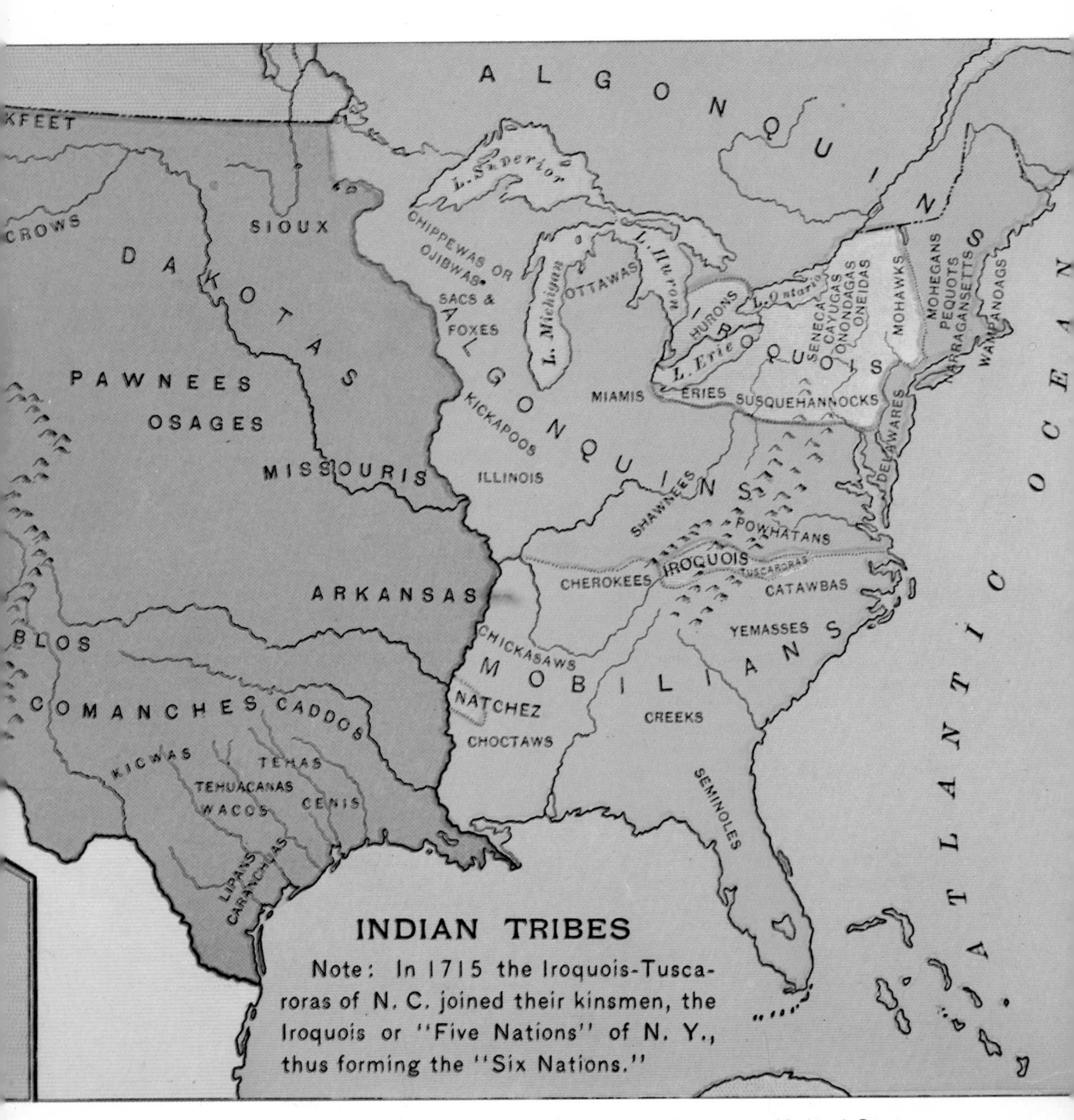

The Mohawks' homeland was in what is now the northeastern United States.

PEOPLE OF THE LAND

The Mohawks call themselves *Kanye Kehá-ka,* a Mohawk word that means "People of the Land of Gun Flint." The homeland of the Mohawk lies near the Hudson River in what is now eastern New York State. Mohawks once traveled from the St. Lawrence River south to Tennessee and west to the Mississippi River.

THE PEACEMAKER

Hundreds of years ago, the Mohawks had a visitor, a peacemaker who told them of a plan for peace. There had been fighting (blood feuds) among the Iroquois for a long time.

The Mohawks were fearless warriors, but they listened to the peacemaker's plan. Five Iroquois tribes made a peace pact. They were the Mohawk, Oneida, Seneca,

This statue, called "Hail to the Sun," is a monument to the Mohawks in Charlemont, Massachusetts.

Onondaga, and Cayuga. The united Iroquois people called themselves the *Haudenosaunee*, which means "People of the Longhouse," because their lands lay next to each other, like families that live under a longhouse roof. The French called them the Iroquois Longhouse or Iroquois Confederacy.

The Haudenosaunee held a great council in a village of the Onondaga nation. Fifty *sachems* (chiefs) attended the council. Nothing could be decided by the council unless all the sachems agreed. The sachems were chosen by clan mothers of the five nations.

Sachems of the Haudenosaunee council meeting with the Europeans

Each nation had several chiefs at the council but only one vote.

Both men and women advised the sachems. If the sachems

did not act in the best interest of the people, they were warned. If they received three warnings and did not change, they were replaced.

Before the "great law" had been adopted, there had been

The Iroquois pipe (above left) and war club (left) are decorated with beads and feathers. Above is a Mohawk mask.

constant war among the Iroquois, Algonquin, and neighboring people.

The Iroquois had forgotten their Creator's words. Before the peacemaker came, warfare was the only way they had to settle quarrels between the people. But when the Haudenosaunee agreed to the Great Law of Peace, the Native Americans learned other ways to settle disputes.

WAMPUM

The Haudenosaunee council chose special tribal members to learn the Great Law. They repeated it over and over until they knew it by heart. The Indians used *wampum* to help them remember, and to record events or to pay for a murder victim.

Wampum was made of beads arranged in special patterns.

If wampum was not

Wampum beads were cut from purple and white clam shells.
A hole was drilled in the middle of each bead.

exchanged at a council meeting, it meant that there was no agreement. Often a

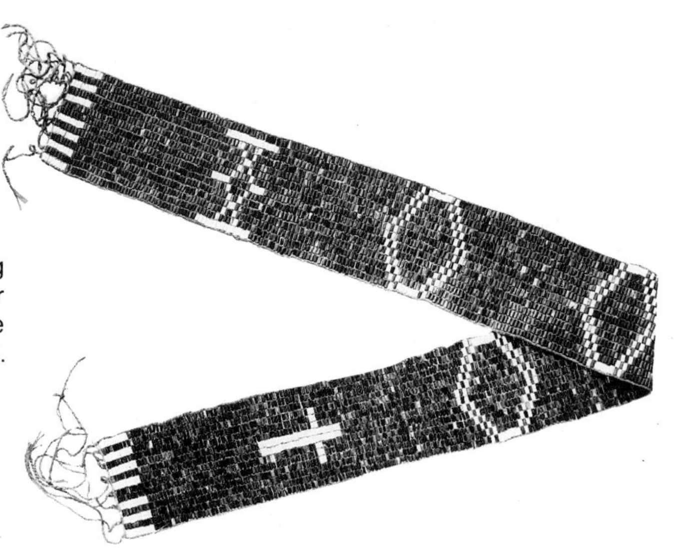

Wampum beads were strung together on leather cords or strings made from plants.

wampum belt was allowed to drop to the ground. This meant no. Sometimes wampum was not even offered. This meant that the next move was up to the hosts of the meeting.

Only trained Indians could interpret wampum. Few people can "read" the

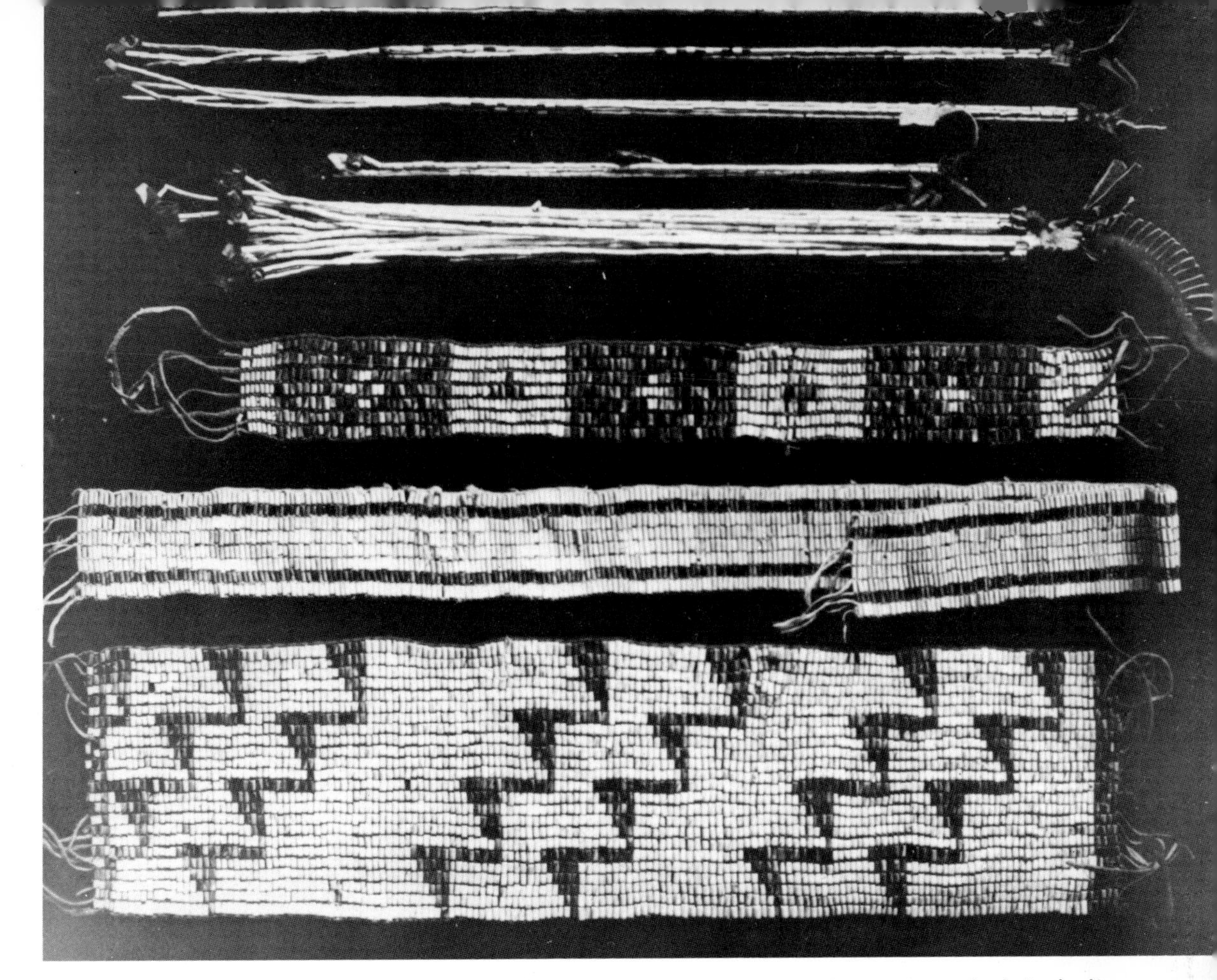

Strings of wampum beads were made into belts.

wampum belts today. Some belts are so old that no living person knows their meaning, but they are still treasured by the tribes.

Benjamin Franklin (left) brought the ideas of the Great Law of Peace to the American colonists. He later invited some sachems to the Constitutional Convention of 1787 (right).

Many ideas in the Constitution of the United States came from the Great Law of Peace. Benjamin Franklin brought these ideas to the colonists who gathered in Albany, New York, in 1754. He also invited Haudenosaunee sachems to the Constitutional Convention.

KEEPERS OF THE EASTERN DOOR

A Mohawk false-face mask

Under the Great Law, the Mohawks were called the Keepers of the Eastern Door because their land lay at the eastern edge of Iroquois territory. If the nation's chiefs failed to reach an agreement, the talks ended. If an agreement was reached by the chiefs, the decision then went to the sachems.

THE CLAN LONGHOUSE

The early Mohawks lived in longhouses that were sometimes 200 feet long! Small elm tree trunks and saplings were used to build frames for these houses. These frames were then covered with tree bark.

Over the doors at each end of the building hung *totems* (emblems) of the Mohawk clan who lived in the longhouse.

The Mohawks had only

The frame of the longhouse was curved to form an arched roof.

three clans—the Turtle, Bear, and Wolf. Under the Mohawk clan system, members of the same clan were related. Members of the same clans in other Iroquois tribes were also relatives. Clan members were always welcomed by their relatives in other villages.

Women of one longhouse were sisters, mothers, or daughters of the same family. When a man married, he moved into his wife's longhouse. Clan mothers

Left: A corn-husk doll. Right: The holes in the longhouse roof let out the smoke from the cooking fires.

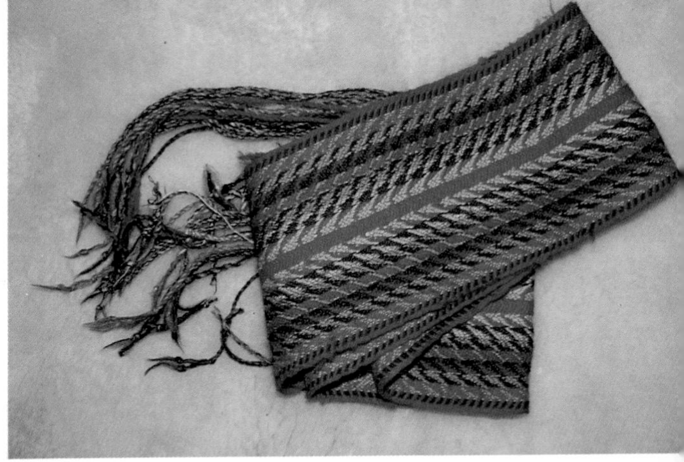

A woven belt (above)
A bowl-and-dice game (left)

arranged marriages for their children. There were no marriages among members of the same clan. Mohawk children were loved and elders were respected. There were no jails, but people could be sent away. Because it was almost impossible to survive in the forest alone, this punishment was almost certainly a death sentence.

Mohawk women raised the crops and prepared and cooked the food.

HOME LIFE

Longhouses stood in clearings surrounded by small farm plots. Forests, marshes, rivers, and lakes covered the rest of the land.

Mohawk women took care of the longhouses, did the farming, and raised the children. The men cleared the fields, hunted, fished, and taught their sons the ways of the woods. Warfare

A Mohawk father (above) teaches his sons to set snares to trap small animals. A clay cooking pot (right)

and defense were also jobs for the men, but required approval of a clan mother.

The Mohawk grew many vegetables and fruits. Like other northeastern tribes, they grew corn, beans, and squash. These vegetables were

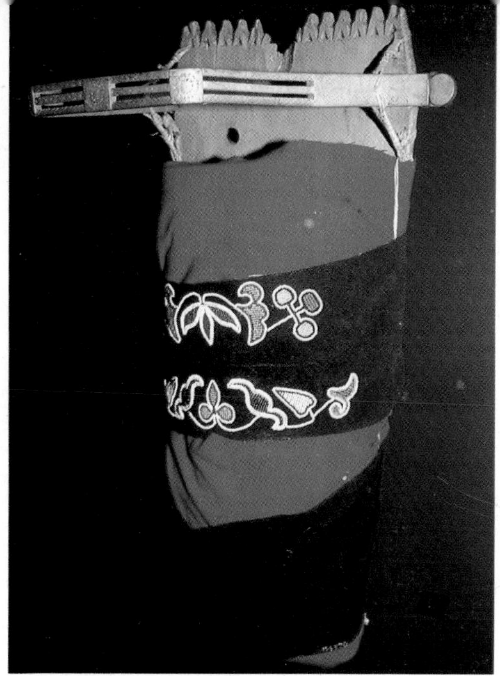

The Mohawks made beautiful decorated baskets (top left). Cradle boards (above) held babies. At left, a bowl and spoons carved from wood.

called the Three Sisters because they were planted together in a mound. The corn would support the vines of the beans and the squash would cover the ground.

CELEBRATIONS

Mohawks respect all living things. Children learn about the Mohawk view of the world through stories. They tell about the sun, thunder, wind, stars, and about the spirits of the plant and animal worlds.

These masks are called "faces of the forest."

Iroquois celebrations include ceremonial dances and traditional songs. In these and other ways, Native Americans give thanks for gifts from the Creator.

One gift from the Creator, according to the Mohawks, is the game known as lacrosse. The Iroquois version of this game was harder to play because there were

Mohawk boys playing lacrosse. This traditional Indian game is played by two teams using webbed rackets with long handles.

few rules. Today, although the game is quite different, it is played with the same spirit.

Snow snake, another traditional game, is still played by the Iroquois.

In this game, a long, polished spear tipped with lead is thrown down an icy track.

The owner and the thrower of the snow snake are a team. The owner polishes the snow snake until it is very slippery. The thrower hurls the snow snake as hard as he can.

Some snow snakes have been clocked at sixty miles per hour. They have slid as far as a mile.

Samuel de Champlain (left) founded the city of Quebec in Canada in 1608. Champlain's soldiers fought a battle with the Iroquois (below) in 1609. Iroquois was the name the French gave to the tribes of the Five Nations.

FOREIGNERS

The French explorer Samuel de Champlain arrived in Canada in 1603. Other explorers later entered the lands of the Mohawks.

In the 1600s and 1700s, the Dutch, French, and English were fighting with one another over their lands in North America. The Mohawks tried to stay out of these fights, but they were caught in the middle.

A sachem (right) holds a wampum belt. Queen Anne of England (below)

Sachems of the three Mohawks clans visited Queen Anne of England in 1710.

Sir William Johnson was known as Johnson of the Mohawks.

Sir William Johnson, an English trader, became very friendly with the Mohawks. They even adopted him into the tribe.

Thayendanegea was also called Joseph Brant.

The Mohawk leader Thayendanegea, also called Joseph Brant, was one of Sir William's closest advisers.

During the American Revolution, Joseph Brant

"took up the hatchet" and fought with the British against the American colonists. Many Mohawks followed him into battle.

When the British were defeated, the Americans moved into Mohawk land. Mohawk villages were destroyed. Finally, the Mohawk people were pushed off their lands.

In appreciation for the loyalty of the Mohawks, the British gave Joseph Brant and his followers land in Akwasasne, high up on the St. Lawrence River. This land was far from their beautiful Mohawk Valley, however. It was also far from the other Haudenosaunee.

A Mohawk town along the St. Lawrence River in Quebec

THE LAND OF AKWASASNE

Akwasasne is a six-mile-square area that lies on both sides of the St. Lawrence River in Canada. Nowadays, not all Mohawks live there,

Mohawk chief Joe Norton stands at the boundary of the Land of Akwasasne.

and not all Indians there are Mohawks. The Mohawk nation is divided, and their government has changed.

Since 1802, one group has elected "trustees." The other group, known as the "traditionals," is trying to continue the old sachem ways.

THE MOHAWK TODAY

Mohawks were among the first Native American people to make the change to an industrial way of life. Mohawk men have become excellent steel and iron workers.

Mohawk iron workers help build skyscrapers.

Single-family houses have replaced the Mohawk longhouse.

Their longhouse life has disappeared. Many Mohawks live as their non-Indian neighbors do—usually in single-family houses. Their children attend public schools.

The Mohawks are still part of the Haudenosaunee. The

ancient Iroquois alliance is very much alive. Sachems are still chosen by the clan mothers, and tribal councils are still held. Today, there is increasing political activity among the "People of the Longhouse."

Mohawks take part in many political marches.

Many countries now recognize the Mohawks and other Iroquois nations as sovereign nations. However, the Mohawk national identity still presents problems for Canada and the United States.

There are probably only half as many Mohawks now as there were in 1534. Disease, guns, alcohol, and oppression have taken a dreadful toll.

Nevertheless, there are still many wise men and

Mohawk leaders of today (left to right):
Christine Taylor, John Montour, and Myrtle Bush

women in the Mohawk nation who are trying to bring peace and prosperity to their people. One of these is Chief Jake Swamp.

Chief Swamp works to save Mother Earth. He has planted trees in many U.S. states and in other countries.

In September 1988, more than two hundred years after the signing of the United States Constitution, Chief Swamp performed a sacred tree-planting ceremony in Washington, D.C. The white pine he planted stands in view of the Lincoln and Vietnam Veterans' memorials. In this way, the men and women of the mighty Haudenosaunee and the

Young Mohawks appear at a rally holding a flag that honors the Native American contribution to North America.

Keepers of the Eastern Door were at last honored for their contributions to democracy in North America.

WORDS YOU SHOULD KNOW

alliance (uh • LYE • ents)—a coming together of different groups for some purpose, such as defense

clan (KLAN)—a group of related families descended from a common ancestor

clearing (KLEER • ing)—an area of land in a forest from which the trees have been cleared

colonists (KAHL • uh • nists)—people who come to live and work in a new country

constitution (kahn • stih • TOO • shun)—a system of basic laws or rules for a government

constitutional convention (kahn • stih • TOO • shun • il kun • VEN • shun)—a meeting called to write a constitution

council (KOWN • sill)—a group of people meeting to discuss plans or to give advice

dispute (diss • PYOOT)—a difference of opinion; disagreement

explorer (ex • PLOR • er)—a person who travels to an unknown part of the world to find out more about it

government (GUV • ern • mint)—a system of ruling a city, state, country, or other group of people

Haudenosaunee (how • den • uh • SAW • nee)—an Iroquois word meaning "People of the Longhouse"

industrial (in • DUSS • tree • il)—having factories and shops; based on manufacturing and trade

Iroquois (EAR • ih • kwoy)—the French name for the tribes of the Five Nations; the Haudenosaunee

lacrosse (luh • KRAWSS)—a ball game played by two teams using webbed rackets with long handles

lead (LED)—a heavy metal

longhouse (LAWNG • **howss**)—a long, narrow dwelling built of poles set in the ground and arched at the top, then covered with sheets of bark

loyalty (LOY • **il** • **tee**)—faithfulness to one's family, country, beliefs, or other meaningful things

matron (MAY • **trun**)—the oldest woman; the woman in charge of a longhouse

oppression (uh • PRESH • **un**)—the cruel use of power; harsh rule

sachem (SAYCH • **im**)—a chief

sapling (SAP • **ling**)—a small, slender young tree

sovereign (SAWV • **rin**)—independent; not subject to another government or people

totem (TOH • **tum**)—an object, such as an animal, serving as a symbol for a family or clan

tradition (truh • DISH • **in**)—highly valued; cherished

tribe (TRYB)—a group of people related by blood and customs

trustees (truss • TEEZ)—persons who occupy positions of trust; representatives of the people who participate in decisions for the group

vengeance (VEN • **jince**)—punishment in return for a harm or injury

wampum (WAHM • **pum**)—small beads made of shells and sewn into patterns on belts, etc.; used by the Indians as money, and to record events

warrior (WOR • **ee** • **er**)—a person trained for fighting; a soldier

INDEX

About the Author

Jill Duvall is a political scientist who received an M.A. from Georgetown University in 1976. Since then, her research and writing have included a variety of national and international issues. Among these are world hunger, alternative energy, human rights, cross-cultural and interracial relationships. One of her current endeavors is a study of ancient goddess cultures. Ms. Duvall proudly serves as a member of the Board of Managers of the Glen Mills Schools, a facility that is revolutionizing methods for rehabilitating male juvenile delinquents.